Usborne First Experiences
Going to the Hospital

Anne Civardi

Illustrated by Stephen Cartwright

Edited by Michelle Bates
Cover design by Neil Francis

Medical adviser: Catherine Sims BSc; MBBS
American consultant: Dr. Lance King

There is a little yellow duck hiding on every double page. Can you find it?

This is the Bell family.

Mr. Bell

Jack and Jill

Mrs. Bell

Ben Bell

Bess Bell

Simba

Ben is six and Bess is three. Ben is not feeling very well.
His ear aches. His ear often aches and it hurts a lot.

Mrs. Bell takes Ben to see Doctor Small.

Doctor Small looks in Ben's ear with an otoscope. He says that Ben needs to have an operation on his sore ear.

Ben has to go to the hospital.

There are lots of other children around. Mrs. Bell helps Ben change his clothes and unpack his suitcase.

He will have his operation later today. He isn't allowed to eat anything for six hours before it.

Ben meets the nurse.

She tucks him up in bed. She takes his temperature and pulse to make sure they are normal.

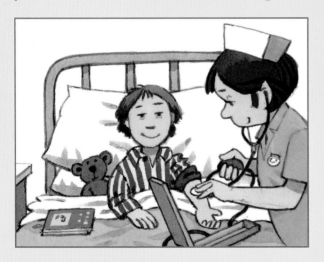 

Then she checks his blood pressure with a special machine. She writes down the results on Ben's chart.

The surgeon comes to see Ben.

She is going to operate on Ben's ear. She tells him what she is going to do, and listens to his heartbeat with a stethoscope.

Ben is ready for his operation.

The nurse comes in to see how Ben is before he is taken to the operating room.

Ben is taken for his operation.

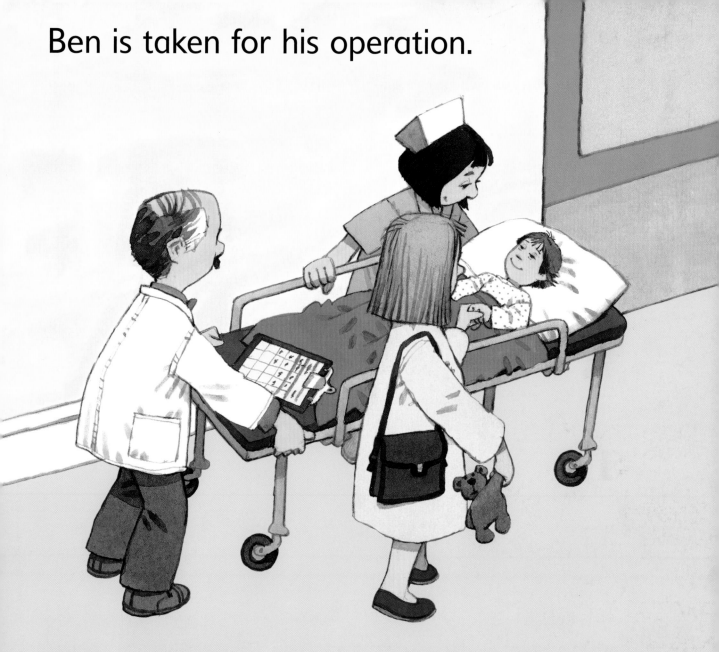

He is wheeled down the long corridors to the operating room. The nurse and Mrs. Bell go with him.

Ben breathes in some gas.

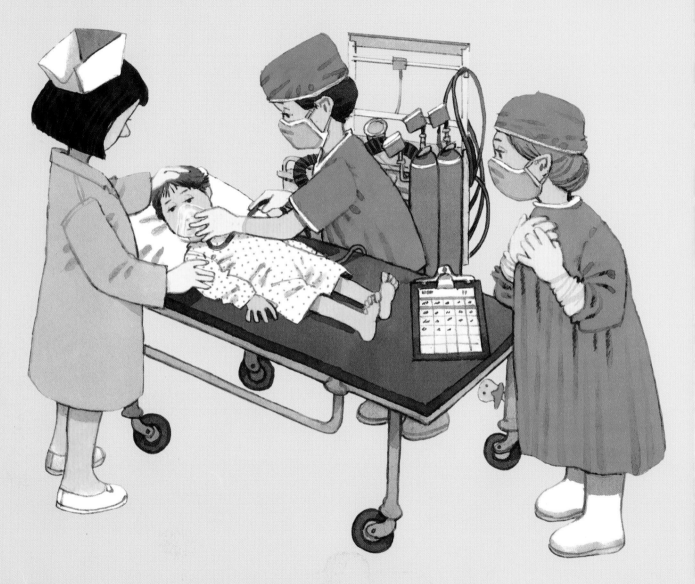

The gas is an anaesthetic which makes Ben sleep soundly during his operation. He has more gas during the operation.

Ben's operation is over.

Ben is taken back to his room. He is still sleepy, but he is pleased to see his mother waiting for him.

Ben goes to the play area.

Ben's ear feels a bit sore, but he feels well enough to get out of bed and play with the other children.

Ben eats lots.

He is very hungry because he hasn't had anything to eat since breakfast.

Ben's family comes to visit him.

Ben is very pleased to see his family, especially his Granny.
Ben shows her his ear. He is very proud of his bandage.

Granny says Ben has been a brave boy and gives him a new toy car. The other children have visitors too.

Ben is ready to go home.

His earache has gone. He says goodbye to the nurse and the surgeon and gives them a big bunch of flowers.

This edition published in 2005 by Usborne Publishing Ltd, Usborne House, 83-85 Saffron Hill, London EC1N 8RT, England.
Copyright © 2005, 1992 Usborne Publishing Ltd. www.usborne.com
First published in America in 2005. UE
The name Usborne and the devices ♀ ⊕ are Trade Marks of Usborne Publishing Ltd.